CIVIL WAR Generals

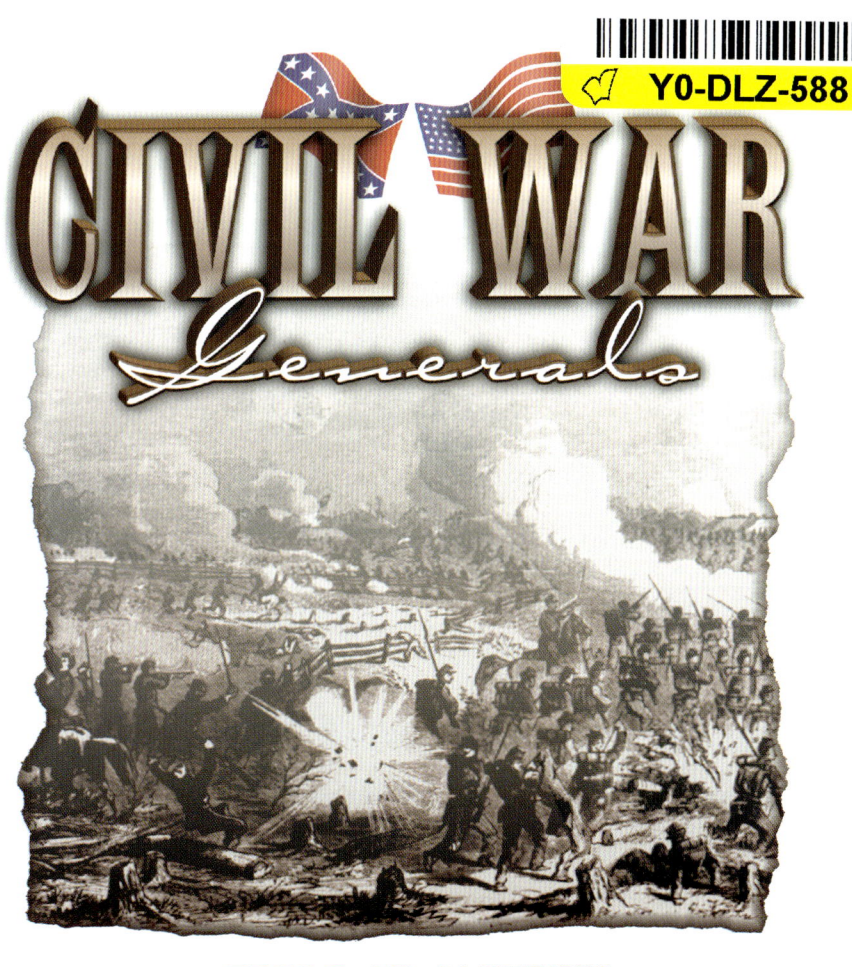

TABLE OF CONTENTS

2	UNION GENERALS
3	ULYSSES SIMPSON GRANT
6	GEORGE BRINTON McCLELLAN
8	PHILIP HENRY SHERIDAN
11	WILLIAM TECUMESH SHERMAN
14	GEORGE HENRY THOMAS
17	CONFEDERATE GENERALS
18	PIERRE GUSTAV TOUTANT BEAUREGARD
21	NATHAN BEDFORD FORREST
24	ROBERT EDWARD LEE
27	JAMES PETER LONGSTREET
30	THOMAS JONATHAN JACKSON

The Union Generals

By virtue of its larger population, the North (Union) never experienced a serious shortage of manpower in comparison to that which plagued the Confederacy. No matter how great its numerical advantage, however, the war would never be won without good military leadership. In this section, the lives and careers of five of the North's most successful officers are detailed. Each of these men played an instrumental part in preserving the Union.

Ulysses Simpson Grant
"Unconditional Surrender"

Born on April 27th 1822 in Point Pleasant, Ohio, Ulysses Simpson Grant is perhaps the best known Union general of the American Civil War. Although he would one day rise to lead vast armies, Grant was a distinctly unlikely candidate for success. He was a failure at almost every venture he undertook in civilian life. The war merely provided him with an opportunity for steady employment. Destiny, however, put Grant on the fast track. Within a few short years, he would go from being a lowly stock clerk in Galena, Illinois to becoming the eighteenth President of the United States.

Grant came from humble beginnings and despite his accomplishments, died a modest man. His true name, Hiram Ulysses Grant, was incorrectly reported to the registrar at West Point. Rather than complain, Grant lived with the mistake and became Ulysses Simpson Grant, after his mother's maiden name of Simpson. The error would one day work to further his career. Newspapers in the North began to refer to him as "Unconditional Surrender" Grant.

In 1843, Grant graduated from West Point a lackluster twenty-first out of a class of thirty-nine. Like most officers in the tiny Federal army of 1860, Grant had served in the Mexican American war. He had fought with Zachary Taylor at Monterey and Winfield Scott at Vera Cruz. Grant's individual bravery garnered official recognition and by war's end, he was promoted to Captain. After the war, he was transferred to garrison duty in California where he apparently "took to the bottle." He received an official reprimand from his commanding officer and soon resigned.

Civilian life held nothing but personal defeats for the hard-working but unlucky farm boy. He tried his hand at a series of occupations, everything from real estate agent to county clerk, but none of these ventures seemed to hold out much promise. When war broke out, he was working as a clerk in a store owned by his two brothers. Grant immediately jumped at the chance to ply his former trade as a military officer.

At length, Grant received a commission to Colonel in June 1861 and was given command of the 21st Illinois Regiment. A few months later, Grant was promoted again, this time to Brigadier General (of Volunteers). Knowing his son's tendency for failure, Grant's father wrote, "Be careful, Ulysses. You're a general now. It's a good job, don't lose it."

Grant's first real success as a military commander was the capture of two Confederate forts in Tennessee; Fort Henry on the Tennessee River and Fort Donelson on the Cumberland. He became a national hero and even had his picture placed on the cover of Harper's Weekly. His uncompromising terms for capitulation won him the nickname that would follow him throughout the war "unconditional surrender."

Grant's next encounter with the enemy was at Shiloh. Here his Army of Tennessee was caught off guard and nearly pushed into the Tennessee River. After being reinforced by divisions from Buell's Army of Ohio, Grant launched a counterattack which drove the Confederates from the field. The casualties at Shiloh were horrendous. Both sides now knew that this would not be a quick and easy war.

For the remaining months of 1862, Grant was preoccupied with capturing Vicksburg, the last remaining Confederate city on the Mississippi River of any consequence. Once Vicksburg fell, southern commerce along the river would be ended and the Confederacy would be split in two. The siege of Vicksburg was one of the most prolonged campaigns of the war. The city finally fell on July 4th 1863 more as a result of widespread starvation and disease than anything else. Lincoln said after Vicksburg, "Grant is my man, and I am his the rest of the war."

Part of what made Grant such an effective officer was his seeming disregard for casualties and reckless nature in comparison to other generals of the day. (McClellan for example.) Upon close inspection however, one finds that Grant was far from callous toward the lives of his men. In addition, his perceived recklessness was in fact merely a preference to take charge of every battle, to wrest the initiative away from his opponent.

Lincoln had long been interested in establishing a unified command system that would coordinate the efforts of all the Union armies east and west. Grant's record for success was such that Lincoln thought he had finally found a general who was up to the task. In March 1864, Grant was brought to Washington at Lincoln's behest. Once there, he received a promotion to Lieutenant General and was appointed to the position of General-in-Chief.

The first major confrontation between Grant and Lee came in May 1864 at a tangled forested area of Virginia known as the Wilderness. In the confused fighting that took place over the next two days, both armies suffered heavy casualties. Instead of retreating, as all previous Union armies had done, the Army of the Potomac continued moving south. Grant and Lee clashed again at Spotsylvania a few days later. Once again the army sustained heavy casualties and no one called for retreat. "I propose to fight it out on this line, if it takes all summer," said Grant in a telegram to Washington. Despite the losses, the men cheered him as a new breed of General, one that would lead them to victory. But as the army drew closer to Richmond, Confederate resistance stiffened. On June 3rd, Grant conducted a massive frontal attack on Confederate entrenchments near Cold Harbor, only six miles from the capitol. It was a disaster even by Civil War standards. Seven thousand Union troops were cut down in as many minutes. Though derided as a butcher back in Washington, Lincoln stuck by Grant.

Grant resumed his outflanking tactics, satisfied that the fortifications around Richmond were too expensive to attack directly. This time he would send his army south, over the James River, and capture Petersburg. Unfortunately, his attack on Petersburg was repulsed at the last moment and another siege ensued.

By early 1865, the end of the Confederacy was close at hand. After stretching Lee's army to the breaking point, Grant was able to enter both Petersburg and Richmond simultaneously. Lee's surrender at Appomattox a few days later was a mere formality.

The war had made a hero out of Ulysses S. Grant. The country hailed him as a military genius and in 1868, it elected him to two terms as President. His administration, however, was beset by corruption, cronyism, and opportunists. Though personally above reproach, Grant nonetheless allowed the illegalities to continue.

After leaving office in 1877, his pre-war period of misfortune returned. Forced to declare bankruptcy, Grant had no choice but to sell his swords and other militaria. He began writing his memoirs to provide income for his family, but it was a race against time. Grant had contracted throat cancer from years of smoking. He died on July 23rd 1885. His memoirs, published by Mark Twain, sold for $450,000.

George Brinton McClellan
"Little Mac"

Born on December 3rd 1826 in Pennsylvania, George B. McClellan is both loved and hated with equal fervor. His superior ability as an administrator enabled him to rebuild the Union army when its fortunes were at low ebb. But, having forged a shiny new weapon, McClellan was reluctant to use it.

George McClellan entered West Point in 1842 at the tender age of fifteen. Despite having difficulty with the "sciences", he went on to graduate second in his class of 1846. The only man to graduate ahead of him, Charles S. Stewart, would one day serve under him as a captain of Engineers. After graduation, McClellan won recognition during the Mexican American War as an officer of engineers.

When Fort Sumter surrendered in April 1861, McClellan was president of the Ohio & Mississippi Railroad. Because of his skill as an administrator and previous military service, the Governor of Ohio appointed him Major General of Ohio volunteers, giving him command of all the state's forces. Soon after, the disaster at Bull Run (Manassas) prompted Lincoln to place McClellan in command of all Union forces east of Ohio.

McClellan's initial concern was to restore some semblance of order and protect the District of Columbia from the counterattack which some believed would occur at any moment. In truth, the Confederate army having won the battle, was just as disorganized and in no shape to conduct an attack. However, in the crisis atmosphere that summer, McClellan played up the threat to enhance his role as savior.

On November 1st, 1861, McClellan was promoted to General-in-Chief of the Armies of the United States. This rapid and heady rise to power had a profound effect on the thirty-five year old. McClellan came to see himself as the savior of the nation and the Army of the Potomac as a tool to fulfill his personal destiny. This dark side of McClellan's character would ultimately manifest itself on the battlefield. Having built a marvelous army, he could not bring himself to risk it in battle.

As Edwin Stanton, Secretary of War put it, "…the champagne and oysters on the Potomac must stop." On March 17th 1862, four months after McClellan assumed command, the army began to move toward Richmond. Rather than approach the Confederate capitol overland, McClellan would move the army by sea to a point of land southeast of Richmond, between the York and the James rivers. The operation would forever be known as McClellan's Peninsula campaign.

Ultimately, the Peninsula campaign failed. Believing himself outnumbered, McClellan halted his army and prepared for a counterattack. The delay was fatal. McClellan advanced at a snail's pace, ever fearful of attack. By the time his army drew close to Richmond, 75,000 rebel soldiers under General Joe Johnston were massed to oppose him. Not content to remain on the defensive, Johnston threw the full weight of his army against McClellan's left wing. The resulting battle of Fair Oaks (Seven Pines) was a murderous mismanaged slugfest. Johnston himself was wounded and replaced by Robert E. Lee.

Lee was determined to drive McClellan away from Richmond and in what came to be called the Seven Day's Battle, his troops savagely attacked and chased the Union army back down the peninsula. In McClellan's own words he had, "…failed to win only because of being overpowered by superior forces." Though none knew it at the time, the Peninsula campaign was over. McClellan returned to Washington, a General without an army, his career seemingly in reverse.

While McClellan took charge of the garrison in Washington D.C., a new army under General John Pope was soundly beaten at the 2nd Battle of Bull Run (Manassas). Pope charged that McClellan had deliberately withheld troops, prompting many to call for his head. Instead of sacrificing him to the mob, however, Lincoln dismissed Pope and had McClellan resume his command.

Having fended off Pope's advance, Lee decided it was time to seize the initiative and invade the North. Unfortunately, a copy of his battle plan (Special Orders 191) fell into Union hands. McClellan now knew the disposition and intentions of Lee's entire army. Moving to intercept the Confederates with uncharacteristic swiftness, McClellan remarked, "Here is a paper with which if I cannot beat Bobby Lee, I will be willing to go home."

As the armies drew closer, McClellan returned to his usual self. He hesitated, estimating Lee's strength as one and a half times his own. The two armies finally met on September 17th, near a tiny creek (Antietam) outside the town of Sharpsburg, Maryland. McClellan could avoid battle no longer and finally gave the word to attack. The battle of Antietam became the bloodiest single day of the entire war.

Though both armies suffered equally, Lee's army lost nearly a third of its strength. The Army of Northern Virginia was crippled and returned to northern Virginia lucky to have escaped. By allowing Lee's army get back to Virginia unmolested, McClellan had sealed his fate.

On November 5th 1862, he was relieved of command and ordered to Trenton, New Jersey. There he sat out the remaining years of the war, criticizing Lincoln's administration and its handling of the war. McClellan was nominated to run for the Presidency against Lincoln in 1864 but his ticket won only three states. He later went on to become Governor of New Jersey, serving from 1878 to 1881.

McClellan died on October 25th 1885 in the midst of writing his memoirs. Having personalized the Army of the Potomac, there can be no denying the positive effect he had on those who served under him. Though unsurpassed as an desk-bound administrator, as an officer he was more concerned with not losing a battle than he was with winning one.

Philip Henry Sheridan
"Little Phil"

Born on March 6th 1831 in Somerset, Ohio, Phillip Henry Sheridan traveled the length of the nation in a military career spanning more than 40 years. He is hailed as a "soldier's soldier," ever aware of his own humble beginnings as the son of an Irish immigrant laborer. Though short in stature, scrappy "Little Phil" Sheridan gained the respect of his men by looking out for their welfare and leading them to victory.

Sheridan came close to wrecking his career in the military before it had a chance to begin. After gaining admission to the West Point class of 1852, he was suspended for a year over an altercation involving another student. He was lucky not to been expelled entirely for this serious breach of discipline. Sheridan's class standing before the incident was not very high and the additional time away from school didn't improve upon his study habits. He finally graduated in 1853, an uninspiring thirty-fourth in his class.

Having earned his commission, Sheridan found himself assigned to duty on the Texas frontier. His poor class standing had made him ineligible for more glamorous assignments. Frontier duty toughened Sheridan, though in truth he probably needed toughening least of all. He remained a Second Lieutenant for nearly eight years, his career at a seeming dead-end. The coming of the American Civil War changed all that.

In April 1861, Sheridan finally got his chance to advance in rank. Now that scores of former classmates were resigning to fight for the Confederacy, officer slots began to open up. He received two promotions in as many months. His first assignment was as Chief Commissary and Quartermaster for the Army of Southwest Missouri. In this capacity, Sheridan was nothing more than a glorified clerk, primarily responsible for making sure that supplies got forwarded to the army.

By all accounts, he served with distinction. Before long, however, Sheridan was clamoring for a front line position and a chance to lead troops in combat. On May 25th 1862, he was promoted to Colonel and given command of the 2nd Michigan Cavalry. Soon after, his troopers uncovered evidence that the Confederate army was massing for an invasion of Kentucky. Thus alerted, the North was able to prepare.

Sheridan's advance warning earned him a promotion to Brigadier General (of Volunteers) in September 1862. Shortly thereafter he participated in the battle of Perryville and was incorrectly reported killed in action. At the battle of Murfreesboro (Stone's River), Sheridan again got advance warning of a Confederate attack and was credited with saving the Union army. On April 10th 1863, newly promoted Major General Sheridan received his second star.

At Chickamauga that September, Sheridan's men suffered very heavy casualties, almost a third of his command. Like the rest of the Union army, the surviving men were fortunate to have escaped this near disaster. Some of his fellow officers later claimed that Sheridan (at the head of his troops) left the field of battle prematurely. This spurious charge was later found to be untrue at least in part. All was forgiven, if not forgotten, months later when Sheridan's men assaulted Missionary Ridge at the battle of Chattanooga and captured the heights. Again, casualties in his command were high accounting for nearly half of the total Union losses suffered at the battle.

In early 1864, Ulysses S. Grant was promoted to Lieutenant General and assumed overall responsibility for the military conduct of war. One of his first acts was to summon Phil Sheridan to Washington and place him in charge of the Army of the Potomac's cavalry corps. Grant made plain his dissatisfaction over his cavalry's performance thus far, especially in comparison to the exploits of Bedford Forrest and J.E.B Stuart's men. Sheridan's mission in coming east, he explained, was to correct this.

Saying that he could "thrash the hell out of Stuart any day," Sheridan quickly proved himself correct. During the subsequent drive on Richmond, while Grant's army bogged down in the Wilderness, Sheridan's men went in search of Confederate cavalry. On May 11th 1864, at Yellow Tavern, they found them. It was a measure of the difference Sheridan had made that Union cavalry could successfully challenge their southern counterparts in the shadow of their own capitol. Sheridan had even made good on his boast. J.E.B Stuart was killed at the battle.

In July, Robert E. Lee sent 15,000 veteran troopers under Jubal Early to raid Washington, D.C. in part to take some pressure off his own men outside Richmond. Although the raid was stopped, it did have one unintended consequence. In August, Sheridan was placed in command of the newly formed Army of the Shenandoah. His mission was to put an end to further such raids, chase after Early's men and in the process, lay waste to their source of supplies the Shenandoah Valley.

Sheridan soon had an opportunity to go after Early's men. At Winchester and Fisher's Hill, his men attacked relentlessly. Though both sides suffered equally in the heavy fighting, the Confederates were forced to retreat eighty miles down the valley. Despite losing nearly 6,000 men in the two battles, Sheridan's army had performed well in its first action.

Sheridan carried out the order to raze the valley with ruthless efficiency. Never again would the Confederates be able to look upon this region as a source of supply or use it as a staging ground for attacks on Washington. Hundreds of barns loaded with crops were burnt in accordance with Grant's wishes that in the future "crows flying over the valley will need to bring their own provisions."

On the night of October 18/19th, Early launched one of the most stunning surprise attacks of the war. Much of Sheridan's army was overrun and sent streaming to the rear. But having won a great victory, Early's men paused to loot the Union camps they captured. This gave Sheridan time to reach the battlefield, take charge of the situation and rally his men by personal example. Union cavalry soon counter-attacked and turned the tide of battle.

Instead of being handed a serious defeat, the battle at Cedar Creek became a high point in Sheridan's career. A poem entitled "Sheridan's Ride" was even written to commemorate the little General's nick-of-time return from Washington. In November, Sheridan received a promotion to Major General (of Regulars) and an official vote of thanks from Congress. Lincoln said of Sheridan, "A cavalryman should be at least six feet four high, but I have changed my mind five feet four will do in a pinch."

Sheridan arrived outside Petersburg in time to take part in the final chapter of the war. At Five Forks and Sayler's Creek, his troops hastened the end by capturing a large portion of Lee's army. Overjoyed at the prospect, he sent Grant his now famous line, "I think if the thing is pressed, Lee will surrender." Lincoln, going over Sheridan's dispatches, replied, "Let the thing be pressed." Lee did surrender within days of this correspondence, in part, because Sheridan's troops were firmly in a position to block Lee's army from escaping.

Sheridan remained on active duty following the war, serving in both Texas and the western Plains. In 1869, when Grant assumed the office of President, "Little Phil" was promoted to Lieutenant General. He was later appointed to General-of-the-Army upon William Sherman's retirement in 1884. It had been quite career. After having spent eight years as a Second Lieutenant, his subsequent rise to the rank of full General was unbelievably swift. Sheridan died on August 5th 1888.

William Tecumseh Sherman
"Uncle Billy"

Born on February 8th 1820 in Lancaster, Ohio, William Tecumseh Sherman is best remembered for his infamous "March to the Sea" and for uttering the simple phrase "war is hell." Sherman is widely regarded by many historians as one of the North's best military leaders, second only to Ulysses S. Grant.

Unlike Grant, however, William Sherman had considerable political connections as a result of his marriage to the daughter of his state Senator (Thomas Ewing). This same senator gained him an appointment to West Point where he graduated sixth in his class of 1840. Other family members, who knew him as "Cump", were equally helpful. His brother John Sherman, for instance, served in Congress for over fifty years.

Sherman fought in the Mexican-American War and although he obtained the rank of Brevet Captain, his term of service was undistinguished. Following the war he left the military to pursue a number of civilian careers (banking and law), all of which ultimately failed. In 1859, Sherman became Superintendent of the Louisiana State Seminary of Learning and Military Academy but his tenure as was short-lived. War broke out less than two years later.

With his country again at war, he re-entered military service as a Colonel and took command of the 13th U.S. Infantry Regiment. Moving up the ranks quickly, he commanded a brigade at the 1st Battle of Bull Run. On August 7th 1861, Sherman was promoted to Brigadier General (of Volunteers) and sent west to help organize Union forces in Kentucky.

Once in Kentucky, his high-strung temperament and outspoken views on the war led many to think him insane. He was relieved of command for insisting, among other things, that the war would only be won by conquest and would require many more men than the 200,000 Lincoln called for. These views conflicted with those who still believed the war would last a mere "90 days." He was transferred to St. Louis under suspicion of being mentally unstable.

In retrospect, the transfer was the best thing that could have ever happened. Though a cloud would hang over his career, he was placed in command of a division under Ulysses S. Grant. This same division would be caught by surprise at the battle of Shiloh. Although his command was largely destroyed, its steadfastness held up the Confederate attack and allowed Grant to eventually win the two day battle.

On May 1st 1862, Sherman received a promotion to Major General (of Volunteers). For the remainder of the year, he was involved with the campaign to close the Mississippi River by capturing Vicksburg. Repulsed at the battle of Chickasaw Bluffs, Sherman's star was again eclipsed for a time. For the second time since coming west, "Uncle Billy" had committed a serious tactical error, the first being his inattentiveness at Shiloh.

U.S. Grant "rescued" his friend however and put him in charge of the XVth Corps. Though he personally opposed Grant's strategy for concluding the siege, Sherman was instrumental in making sure it succeeded. Vicksburg fell on July 4th 1863. With the city now in Union hands, Sherman's men chased the remaining Confederate troops out of central Mississippi. Following this success, he received his first "regular army" field grade promotion to Brigadier General.

For the next several months, Sherman and his corps was temporarily without a job. As outspoken as ever, he used the respite as an opportunity to compose his thoughts on the war. Victory would come, he believed, only after "we remove and destroy every obstacle, if need be, take every life, every acre of land, everything that to us seems proper." Moreover, he remarked, "I would make this war as severe as possible and show no symptoms of tiring till the South begs for mercy… The South has done her worst, and now it is time for us to pile on our blows thick and fast."

Sherman was soon to get his chance to pile on blows. Late in 1863, he participated in the battle of Missionary Ridge which freed the Union army trapped within Chattanooga and started the drive toward Atlanta. Unable to stop the advancing Union army, southern guerrillas and Bedford Forrest's mounted raiders began disrupting its supply columns in the rear. Sherman was prepared to deal with this harassment with a show of force even if it included making war on civilians. "War is cruelty," he said, "There is no use trying to reform it. The crueler it is, the sooner it will be over."

In March 1864, Grant was promoted to Lieutenant General and brought to Washington to oversee the conduct of the entire war. With Grant now in charge, Sherman was given command of the West. Grant's recipe for ending the war, as Sherman later explained, was that Grant should go after Lee's army in Virginia while he (Sherman) was to defeat Joe Johnston and deliver the city of Atlanta before the November elections.

By outflanking the Confederate positions rather than attacking them head on, Sherman methodically closed in on Atlanta. Rather than create another Vicksburg, Sherman swung his army around the city to cut off its supply line. His men tore up railroad tracks by heating the iron rails then twisting them around nearby trees. The iron loops came to be known as "Sherman's neckties."

On September 3rd, Sherman's men marched into Atlanta, the first major southern city to fall into Union hands since the taking of New Orleans. It was the crowning achievement of the campaign and gave Lincoln the victory he desperately needed. Sherman, now a Major General of Regulars, proposed to move his army east from Atlanta to Savannah.

Sherman began his legendary "March to the Sea" on Nov 15th 1864 intent upon demonstrating that his army could move throughout the south at will. Promising to "make Georgia howl," he encouraged his men to "forage liberally." In truth, it was a license to loot and pillage. He reached Savannah in mid-December At a cost of less than 1,000 men, his army inflicted over $100 million in damage. Georgia was out of the war.

Having proven his army's ability to operate independently behind enemy lines, Sherman was asked to march north from Savannah toward Virginia, wreaking the same kind of havoc through the Carolinas as he had in Georgia. By mid March, his army was in North Carolina less than 50 miles from Richmond. Caught between Sherman and Grant, Lee's army was forced to evacuate both Richmond and Petersburg early in April. On April 9th, Lee surrendered near Appomattox creek, ending the war for all practical purposes.

Sherman was one of the first officers to understand the implications of waging a "modern war." He knew that to win a war the enemy must be beaten on the home front as well as on the battlefield. Though his views caused many to believe him insane, by war's end he was more than vindicated. Never a particularly skilled tactician, he was energetic and not afraid to take risks. Sherman finally retired from active duty in 1884, not quite twenty years after his taking of Atlanta and subsequent "march to the sea." He died in New York on February 14th 1891.

George Henry Thomas
"Rock of Chickamauga"

Born on July 31st 1816, in Virginia, George Henry Thomas' achievements are often overlooked next to more recognizable figures like Grant or Sherman. Much about Thomas remains private. Though sincerely modest and reserved, Thomas' reluctance to discuss his affairs likely stems from the fact that being born a southerner, he turned his back on family and friends to fight for a cause.

Thomas' first contact with the military came in 1836 when he gained entrance to West Point. His admission came about by virtue of his family and their political connections. Thomas graduated twelfth in his class (1840) the same class in which William T. Sherman finished sixth. An artilleryman by trade, he was posted to various coastal batteries after graduation.

He fought with distinction in the Mexican American war and received a promotion to Major. Following the war, he was stationed in Texas and served with the 2nd Cavalry amongst a number of officers he would one day take up arms against. (The list includes Albert Sidney Johnston, Robert E. Lee, and William Hardee.) He was severely wounded in 1860 while fighting along the Indian frontier in Texas.

In January 1861, he applied for the position of Commandant of Cadets at the Virginia Military Institute (VMI). This led many people to conclude that he was pro-secessionist. He was after all, from Virginia, and had been forced to flee Nat Turner's slave rebellion in 1836. However, when the time came to choose between Virginia and his allegiance to the United States, Thomas choose the latter. Within weeks of Fort Sumter, Thomas was promoted to Colonel.

Thomas spent the first few months of the war in the Shenandoah valley. He was quickly promoted to Brigadier General (of Volunteers) after the Bull Run campaign. With McClellan taking charge of the army in Washington, Thomas was sent to Kentucky. In January 1862, he attacked and destroyed a small Confederate force near Mill Springs. Any lingering doubts as to his loyalty were removed at the news of this victory.

Following Mill Springs, Thomas was posted to Don Carlos Buell's Army of the Ohio. He was present at the battle of Shiloh though took no active command role. Soon after, he was promoted to Major General (of Volunteers). Buell, like McClellan, could not move fast enough to suit those in Washington. When he was forced to respond to a Confederate invasion of Kentucky, Lincoln asked Thomas to replace Buell. Thomas declined the offer on the basis that it was bad policy to remove a General on the eve of battle (Perryville).

Though Thomas had rendered competent service as a subordinate at both Perryville and Stone's River (Murfeesboro), it wasn't until the battle of Chickamauga that he finally gained the recognition he deserved. This particularly brutal fight came close to destroying the Union Army of the Cumberland had it not been for Thomas' steadfast determination to hold his ground. His stubborn defense earned him the sobriquet "Rock of Chickamauga."

When Grant assumed command of all western forces in October 1863, one of his first actions was to put Thomas in charge of the army he had "saved" at Chickamauga. Now at the head of his own army for the first time in the war, Thomas was to participate in the drive on Atlanta. It was Thomas' men who, acting on their own initiative, pushed the Confederates off their entrenchments atop Missionary Ridge and got the campaign started. When the Confederates launched a counterattack outside Atlanta, it was Thomas' men who stopped them.

After Atlanta fell in September, Sherman was chomping at the bit to start his infamous "March to the Sea." Washington was reluctant to let him go, however, because scattered Confederate forces in Alabama and Mississippi threatened to sever his line of communications. As a compromise, Sherman split his force sending Thomas west to Nashville along with two corps while he himself headed east toward Savannah.

As expected, a Confederate army under General John B. Hood began moving into Tennessee. Though heavily outnumbered, Hood hoped to force Sherman to call off his march through Georgia. In late November, Hood attacked a portion of Thomas' men at Franklin, just south of Nashville. The battle was a very bloody affair in which no less than twelve southern Generals were killed, wounded, or captured.

Although his troops had won the battle, Thomas had them withdraw to Nashville where the rest of his army was waiting. Foolishly Hood followed. Thomas was content to let the Confederates sit outside the city while he prepared a counter-attack. He moved with such "McClellan-esque" deliberation, however, that outside observers thought Thomas was missing a golden opportunity. Grant even went so far as to recommend to Lincoln that he be removed from command. By the time the order removing Thomas from command was sent, Thomas had launched his counterattack and smashed the rebel army.

The battle of Nashville was one of the few times in the war that an army was almost entirely destroyed. After the battle, Thomas gained a new nickname "the Sledge of Nashville." From "Rock" to "Sledge," he had proven his generalship. Known for being excellent on defense, Thomas showed he could fight aggressively as well. Grant's order removing him from command was forgotten and on January 16th 1865, Thomas was promoted to Major General.

It was once said of Thomas," There are two types of eminent men we are frequently called upon to study. In one, we are amazed at the man for having achieved what was claimed for him; in the other, we are astonished that he did not accomplish more. In this latter class, George Henry Thomas stands conspicuous."

Though Thomas does not have the same level of name-recognition as Grant or Sherman, he was instrumental in helping them achieve success. While Sherman stumbled at Missionary Ridge, Thomas' men stormed the heights. At a time when Grant was calling for his dismissal, Thomas was busy planning what would ultimately be the most resounding one-sided victory of the war.

Thomas remained in command of the Department of the Tennessee until 1867. Unfortunately, he became embroiled in a political skirmish between President Andrew Johnson and U.S. Grant. He asked for, and received, reassignment to the Department of the Pacific. He remained on active duty in San Francisco until his death on March 28, 1870.

The Confederate Generals

When the American Civil War began in April 1861, the South's chances of winning independence looked bleak. On paper, the military and industrial strength of the North was overwhelming. Not only did the North have a larger population and greater industrial base, it also had a vastly superior railroad system and access to abundant raw materials. Only in the area of military leadership did the Confederacy hold a significant advantage. True, this advantage would gradually erode in time but the quality of its general staff was the one intangible that kept the South from simply being overrun. In this section, the lives and careers of five of these men are detailed, showing in part, how their battlefield successes very nearly won the war.

Pierre Gustav Toutant Beauregard
"Napoleon in Gray"

Born on May 28th, 1818 in Parish Louisiana, Pierre Gustav Toutant Beauregard, is one of the more colorful characters of the American Civil War. It was his command that fired the first shots at Fort Sumter and it was he, along with Joe Johnston, who surrendered the last major Confederate army in 1865. Never very far from a fight, Beauregard served continuously, from beginning to end, in every major theater of the war. Though his relationship with Jefferson Davis was sometimes strained, this dashing Creole was extremely popular with the average southerner.

Beauregard was born into luxury. His parents considered themselves aristocrats, part of the slave-owning plantation class of the Old South. His parents wanted him to grow up in the French tradition and sent him, at age eleven, to study at the "French School" in New York City. While attending this school, young Beauregard delighted in stories about Napoleon Bonaparte told to him by his instructors, former officers in la Grande Armee. He soon asked his father to secure him an appointment to West Point.

Beauregard entered the West Point academy in 1834 at age sixteen. Though English was his second language, Beauregard excelled in his studies throughout his four year stay. He graduated second out of a class of forty-five. Though intelligent, he was also hot-headed and keenly sensitive to insults to his "honor." Once, while serving as a 2nd Lieutenant of Engineers, he challenged another officer to a duel with shotguns. Only the timely intervention by the local sheriff prevented the match from taking place.

When America went to war against Mexico in 1846, like most officers, Beauregard saw it as an opportunity for quick advancement. Though only a Brevet Captain, he was asked by the commanding General (Winfield Scott) to present his views on the attack on Mexico City. His plan was to attack Chapultapec and enter Mexico City from the west. Though many of Scott's senior officers disagreed, the

General was impressed by the young Captain's confident manner. Beauregard's plan was ultimately adopted.

In January 1861, Beauregard was appointed Superintendent of West Point by virtue of his military service and certain important political connections he made along the way. But being from Louisiana, Beauregard made clear his intention to resign if his home state voted to leave the Union. As a result, he earned the distinction of having the shortest tenure (23 to 28 January) of any Superintendent.

Beauregard headed back to Louisiana. Upon being told that the top state command was going to Braxton Bragg, he enlisted as a private in the Orleans Guard (13th Louisiana). This act of false bravado was as dramatic as it was insincere. Beauregard had no intention of fighting the war as a private. When Jefferson Davis asked him to take command of the forces opposite Fort Sumter, he hurriedly left his native state and went to South Carolina. Beauregard would remain on the Orleans Guard roster as "absent on duty" for the duration of the war.

Fort Sumter fell to Beauregard's guns after a short bombardment. Ironically, the Union officer in charge of the garrison was one of his former instructors at West Point. Though the taking of the fort was more show than substance, it made good copy. The first shot of the war had been fired, a victory had been won, and the name Beauregard would become a household word.

With Virginia in the war, the "hero" of Sumter was now needed to plan for the defense of Richmond, the new capitol of the Confederacy. Given his aristocratic French ancestry, it's understandable that southerners would go so far as to invite comparisons between Beauregard and Napoleon Bonaparte. Jefferson Davis summoned his "Napoleon in Gray" to Virginia and put him in command of some forces there.

Beauregard's first major battle (Manassas) was a bit of a muddle. Neither the officers nor the men were properly prepared. It was Confederate victory but it could easily have gone the other way. Even before the battle started, however, Beauregard was miffed at being placed in a subordinate position to General Joe Johnston. Now that he had a second victory under his belt, Beauregard felt confident enough to begin accusing the Davis administration of mismanaging the war. He was promoted then sent west.

Once again, Beauregard was placed "second in command," this time serving under General Albert Sidney Johnston. After Johnston's death on the first day at Shiloh, Beauregard assumed responsibility for the army. Finally, he had what he had always sought independent command. It was Beauregard who made the final decision to withdraw, all the while announcing that a great victory had been won.

Beauregard retained command of the army for several months after Shiloh but came under sharp criticism for not crushing the enemy as had been promised. Not only had a great victory not been won, his army was apparently unable to even hold its ground. Davis relieved the Creole from command. In September 1862, Beauregard headed back to Charleston to take command of the forces there. His primary responsibility would be to defend the Atlantic seaboard of South Carolina and Georgia.

Undoubtedly, the move was a good one for both Beauregard and the Confederacy. As popular as the General was with the public, he had fallen out of favor with members of government including Jefferson Davis himself. Thus far, he had shown little in the way of Napoleonic prowess on the battlefield, tending instead to devote his time to conjuring up impractical grand strategies. His hair had turned completely gray, not from stress as one might imagine, but due to the Union blockade cutting off the supply of dye.

Being an engineer by trade, Beauregard set about strengthening the harbor defenses. He asked for, and received, additional troops. At the same time, his area of responsibility was increased to as far south as Florida. In January 1863, he won a small naval engagement which succeeded in driving off the blockading Union vessels for a time. Beauregard quickly announced that the blockade had been lifted, but in truth, it had not. Union ships would resume their patrol outside Charleston harbor within days

Despite his success in protecting Charleston, the on-going war of words with Jefferson Davis threatened to keep Beauregard on the sidelines while other officers took a more active role. Davis would never again give him independent command of an army in the field. By the spring of 1864, however, Beauregard's popularity was never higher.

As Lee's army began falling back on Richmond that summer, Beauregard was ordered to take charge of the troops moving into Petersburg. For the first time in the war, Lee was unsure of his opponent's intentions and lost track of the Union army. By guessing that the Union army would bypass Richmond and head for Petersburg instead, Beauregard managed to save both the city, and Lee's reputation.

The defense of Charleston in 1863 and Petersburg in 1864 showed Beauregard at his best but his poor relationship with Davis kept his dream of an independent command from being fulfilled. Uncomfortable being a mere corps commander under Lee, Beauregard wanted out of Virginia. Davis offered him a new position as head of the Military Department of the West. In this capacity, he would take charge of all Confederate forces from Georgia to the Mississippi River.

Beauregard readily accepted the new position only to find out that it was largely administrative with no real power. Much to his chagrin, Beauregard was stuck as a behind-the-scenes advisor, a one man fire brigade to be shifted from one crisis to another. He was present as Sherman entered Savannah, with Hood as his shattered army fell back from Nashville, and finally would accompany Joe Johnston at his surrender in North Carolina.

Looking back, it was Beauregard's lot in life to forever be second in command. Though he held out great promise, his intemperate comments concerning the government and Jeff Davis doomed his career. Right until the end of the war, many in the south considered him to be their "Napoleon in Gray," something Beauregard did little to discourage. Except for an occasional flourish, however, he did little to deserve the title. He died in New Orleans on February 20th 1893.

Nathan Bedford Forrest
"The Wizard of the Saddle"

Born on July 13th 1821 in Bedford County, Tennessee, Nathan Bedford Forrest is one of the most colorful characters of the American Civil War. In daring, dash, and innate military acumen, he is unsurpassed by any other military leader, North or South. Many consider him to be the preeminent cavalryman of the war and epitome of the southern fighting man. Forrest personally killed thirty-two men in combat, more than any other general officer, and had thirty-three horses shot from underneath him. With typical aplomb, Forrest remarked that by the end of the war he "was a horse ahead."

Of the South's senior general officers, only Bedford Forrest was without a college education. At the start of the war, however, he was one of the richest. Barely literate, Forrest amassed a personal fortune from shrewd dealing in farm supplies and slaves. Shortly after enlisting as a private in the 7th Tennessee Cavalry, he was promoted to Lieutenant Colonel and charged with raising his own battalion of troops.

In October 1861, Lt. Col. Forrest was elected to lead a 500 man cavalry unit (mounted rangers). In their first operation, Forrest's men were rushed to the defense of Fort Donelson, then under siege by General Grant. Upon their arrival, they learned that the garrison was on the verge of surrendering. Saying that they had not ridden all this way just to become prisoners of war, Forrest led his men back through the Union lines and escaped.

After the fall of Donelson and subsequent surrender of Fort Henry, Forrest was ordered to join the mass of Confederate troops assembling at Corinth. His troops took part in the surprise attack on Union troops near Shiloh shortly thereafter. The attack was repulsed with heavy loss of life, however, and Forrest himself was wounded at the battle.

General P.G.T Beauregard soon became a great admirer of the "unlettered" officer. He persuaded Forrest to go Chattanooga and take charge of the disorganized Confederate cavalry there. Promised a promotion to Brigadier General, Forrest left for Tennessee and assumed command of a brigade. He celebrated his birthday by successfully attacking the Union garrison at Murfreesboro and in an effort to "out-Grant" Grant, Forrest levied a "surrender or die" ultimatum. The garrison wisely accepted.

Days later, Forrest received his promotion. His rise through the ranks, from Private to Brigadier General, was remarkable. He had gained notoriety for audacity and heroism, yet his operations were calculated and conducted with common sense. Given the type of "hit and run" tactics being employed, Forrest was fast developing a reputation as a guerrilla fighter.

Forrest's operations in Tennessee continued throughout the spring of 1863. His skirmishing and "behind-the-lines" harassment caused no end of consternation. No one ever knew quite where or when his men would strike. As a result, Union manpower that could be better used in the front lines was frittered away garrisoning supply depots and railroads.

Even so, the North had enough strength to advance on both Vicksburg and Atlanta simultaneously. In support of these campaigns, Union cavalry conducted two large scale raids of their own. To support Grant's effort at Vicksburg, a brigade was sent from Tennessee south through Mississippi, tearing up Confederate railroads along the way. The second raid, led by Colonel Abel Streight, was aimed at cutting the railroad running between Atlanta and General Braxton Bragg's army near Chattanooga.

To the misfortune of those involved, Streight's troopers ran into a detachment of Forrest's cavalry. Though heavily outnumbered, Forrest kept in constant contact with Streight's column. Forced to fight at every turn, the Union cavalry tired quickly and was eventually brought to heel far short of their objective. Thinking quickly, Forrest was able to convince Streight that he was surrounded by superior numbers. Streight surrendered his force of nearly 2,000 men to Forrest, who at the time, had less than 600 men present on the field.

In February 1864, Forrest's men intercepted a force of 7,000 Union cavalrymen, under Col. W Sooy Smith, moving south from Memphis. Forrest had less than half as many men but his cavalry soon fought the Union column to a standstill. Unfortunately, his youngest brother, Jeffrey a Colonel in one of his brigades, was killed in the fighting. Smith, believing himself to be outnumbered, turned and ran back to Memphis with Forrest in hot pursuit.

In March, Forrest used the same ruse he had used against Streight, with similar results. By an ironic twist of fate, his 7th Tennessee Cavalry bluffed an entire Union regiment into surrendering at Union City. The surrendering regiment turned out to be the 7th Tennessee Cavalry (Union). From here, Forrest's men moved north to Fort Pillow and tried the same bluff a third time. It didn't work this time. Forrest was forced to assault the fort. The resulting "massacre" remains controversial today.

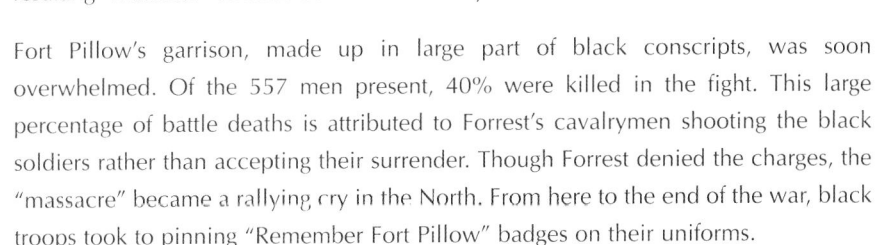

Fort Pillow's garrison, made up in large part of black conscripts, was soon overwhelmed. Of the 557 men present, 40% were killed in the fight. This large percentage of battle deaths is attributed to Forrest's cavalrymen shooting the black soldiers rather than accepting their surrender. Though Forrest denied the charges, the "massacre" became a rallying cry in the North. From here to the end of the war, black troops took to pinning "Remember Fort Pillow" badges on their uniforms.

Soon after Fort Pillow, Forrest won his greatest victory of war at a place called Brice's Crossroads. In June 1864, his command attacked a mixed force of Union infantry and cavalry led by General Samuel Sturgis. Though the enemy had superior numbers (as usual), Forrest correctly surmised that bad weather in the area would prevent the infantry from keeping up with the mounted troops. With the Union forces divided, he would have an opportunity to defeat them in detail. At a cost of some 500 men, Forrest sounded defeated Sturgis, taking 1,600 of his men prisoner along with 18 cannon and 175 supply wagons.

Having quickly reached the pinnacle of his military career, Forrest was about to experience a stunning reversal of fortune. The following month, a similar expedition led by Major General Andrew Smith, left Memphis with orders to suppress Forrest and his gray-back cavalry. At Tupelo, Mississippi, Forrest's cavalry assaulted the Union troops but were repulsed with heavy losses. Four of his brigades were so completely shattered as to be rendered combat ineffective for the remainder of the war.

After his drubbing at Tupelo, Forrest went back to staging small guerrilla raids. By now, however, Sherman was not to be stopped. Atlanta would fall before the November elections. Although he participated in General John B. Hood's Franklin and Nashville campaign, Forrest's tiny force was used primarily as scouts. In April 1865, the few men he had left were pursued by Union cavalry and destroyed near Selma, Alabama.

Forrest somehow managed to survive the war despite being in the thick of battle for four long years. Although his slave dealing days were over, he returned to a successful farming business and eventually became President of the Marion & Memphis Railroad. In time, he would become "Grand Wizard" of the Ku Klux Klan. While this virulent racism detracts from Forrest's character as a man nothing can take away from his success as a military leader. He died in Memphis on October 29th 1877.

Robert Edward Lee
"Bobby Lee"

Born on January 19th 1807 in Virginia, Robert Edward Lee was the epitome of the fine bred southern gentlemen. He was also one of the greatest military leaders to take part in the American Civil War. Though he personally was not a slave owner, Lee was willing to fight for the institution because it meant defending his native state. From 1861 to 1865, Lee's fortunes and those of his country would be irrevocably entwined. It is largely due to his skill as a military officer that the Confederacy survived as long as it did.

Robert E. Lee was the fifth son of Major General Henry "Light Horse Harry" Lee, a distinguished cavalry officer and aide to George Washington. Henry Lee, it is remembered, is known for delivering the famous eulogy "He was first in war, first in peace, first in the hearts of his countrymen." Henry Lee died early in young Robert's life, having lost a great deal of the family's fortune in land speculation.

Despite his family's poor financial situation, Lee obtained an appointment to West Point in 1825. He proved to be an excellent student, graduating second in his class without a demerit on his record. Lee received a commission as a 2nd Lieutenant of Engineers and served at a number of southern coastal fortifications in this capacity. In 1831, Lee married Mary Anna Randolph Custis, a granddaughter of Martha Washington. In time, he and Mary would have three sons, all of whom would one day serve in their father's army.

When the Mexican-American War erupted in 1846, Captain Lee was dispatched to Texas as an officer of Engineers. Later, Lee would take part in the Vera Cruz campaign under General Winfield Scott. His distinguished service during the advance on Mexico City won official recognition in the form of a brevet promotion to Colonel. From 1852 to 1855, Colonel Lee served as Superintendent of West Point. While serving as Superintendent he extended the course of study there from four years to five.

It was Lee who took John Brown into custody following his failed attempt to lead a slave uprising in October 1859. Brown's raid on Harper's Ferry is often cited as a catalyst for the Civil War. As the pace of events leading to war accelerated in 1860, Winfield Scott "Old Fuss and Feathers" recommended that Lee be offered command of the Union army. Lee politely refused. Although he personally held slavery to be a "moral and political evil", he found himself unable to take up arms against his home.

Lee resigned his commission from the US Army on April 20th 1861, days after Virginia voted to secede from the Union. Having said "I am one of those dull creatures that cannot see the good of secession", Lee returned to home to take command of Virginia's military forces. As much as he would one day accomplish, Lee's career was slow to take off. After being promoted to Brigadier General in the regular army, he was sent to inspect the shore defenses along the Atlantic seaboard. In March 1862, Lee returned to Richmond and served as a military advisor to Jefferson Davis.

When General Joe Johnston was wounded at the battle of Seven Pines (Fair Oaks) Davis replaced him with an officer who thus far had failed to distinguish himself as a successful field commander Robert E. Lee. Upon learning of this change in command George McClellan remarked, "I prefer Lee to Johnston. The former is too cautious and weak under grave responsibility. Personally brave and energetic to a fault, he yet is wanting in moral firmness when pressed by heavy responsibility, and is likely to be timid and irresolute in action." Lee would soon give McClellan ample cause to take back these words.

The Army of Northern Virginia quickly became Lee's personal army in much the same way as the Army of the Potomac was McClellan's. But unlike McClellan, Lee and his army drew close as partners in adversity are apt to do. Outnumbered by the massive Union host, Lee's men understood the principle of desperate times calling for desperate measures. Their attacks during the Seven Days battles were driven home with a ferocity which shook the Union army.

By capitalizing on McClellan's sluggish nature, Lee forced the Union General to give up his Peninsula campaign. This ability to "read" his opponent was in part, a secret of his success. Lee was familiar with many of the Union officers he would face over the next four years. As a result, he could often divine their intentions and use this knowledge to defeat them. Late in the war, Lee would express the fear that Lincoln would keep changing Generals until he got one that Lee wouldn't understand.

In August 1862, Lee defeated McClellan's successor (John Pope) at the 2nd battle of Manassas (Bull Run). A month later, McClellan was back in command. After discovering a detailed copy of Lee's plan to invade the North, McClellan allowed himself to be fought to a standstill at the battle of Sharpsburg (Antietam). Lee lost a third of his army at this "Shiloh of the East" and was forced to call off his invasion. At year's end, Lee made the most of Ambrose Burnside's ineptitude at Fredericksburg, saving Richmond for a third time.

As the war entered its third year, Lee recognized that the Confederacy was fast reaching the end of its available manpower. Though he had fought his most masterful contest yet, defeating Joe Hooker at Chancellorsville, Lee believed that if the South was going to win the war it had to strike a devastating blow on Northern soil. This proved to be Lee's undoing.

Lee followed up his victory over Hooker with a second northern foray. Ill-served by his subordinates, Lee was forced to fight the most important battle of the war, with little knowledge of the enemy and on unfamiliar ground. The battle of Gettysburg (July 1st - 3rd) was a disaster. Lee wrecked his Army of Northern Virginia during three days of headlong charges at prepared Union positions. The flower of his army was now gone, and with it, all chance to end the war by offensive action. After Gettysburg, Lee would never again fight a major campaign on enemy soil.

Though Gettysburg was a turning point in the war, it did not dash all hopes of victory. Many in the South believed that the Confederacy could still win by inflicting grievous casualties on the North and wear down its resolve to continue. Some even held out the chance that some European power might intervene on their behalf. In short, Lee could still win, if he could keep from losing. Richmond was the key, and both sides knew it.

Unfortunately, just as Lee had feared, Lincoln finally found his man in the person of Ulysses S. Grant. After clashing at the Wilderness in May 1864, Lee realized that Grant could not be goaded into retreating like all his predecessors. "Grant will fight us every hour, every day, until the end of the war." Though Lee remained at the top of his game, showing the same tactical skill as always, he was not able to deal with an opponent willing to fight to the last man.

In the end, Grant's superior numbers proved too much. Lee's army was forced into static defenses around Richmond and Petersburg. There it remained until the very last days of the war. In April 1865, after evacuating Richmond and Petersburg, Lee surrendered the tattered remnants of his army at Appomattox Court House.

After his parole, Lee devoted the remaining years of his life to running Washington College in Lexington, Virginia. His wartime exploits made him a legendary figure of the Civil War and a symbol of the Confederacy. He died on October 12th 1870, leaving the country with an enduring legacy of bravery and selfless devotion.

James Peter Longstreet
"Old Pete"

Born on January 8th 1821 in South Carolina, James Longstreet was one of most able and trusted officers in the Confederacy. He fought in many different places under a variety of commanders but Longstreet's greatest success came while serving at the head of a corps in Robert E. Lee's Army of Northern Virginia. Despite his long years of service and reputation as a brilliant tactician, Longstreet ended his days a controversial figure. Many in the South held him responsible for the defeat at Gettysburg a charge that would follow him to his grave.

Like a number of other officers, Longstreet obtained his appointment to West Point through his family's political connections. By all accounts, he was not a good student and struggled through his four years at the Academy. Ironically, one of Longstreet's best friends was another cadet, Ulysses S. Grant. It was Longstreet who introduced Grant to Julia Dent, the woman Grant would one day marry.

Upon his graduation in 1842, he was commissioned as a Second Lieutenant and served on the Indian frontier. He was also present at the storming of Monterey during the Mexican-American war. After Fort Sumter surrendered in April 1861, Major Longstreet resigned his commission and returned to his home state. Within months, he had been appointed Brigadier General in the Confederate army.

Longstreet's first taste of action came at the battle of Manassas (Bull Run) in July 1861. Posted on the right flank of the Confederate, his men held their positions throughout the battle. Following the battle, Longstreet was promoted to Major General.

In March 1862, Longstreet was involved in stopping McClellan's Peninsula campaign from taking Richmond. His message to his troops was simple, "Keep cool, obey orders, and aim low." Outside Richmond, Longstreet would demonstrate his natural ability as a defensive fighter. At the same time, a case could be made that the General was uncomfortable in an offensive role. His preferred way to make war was to allow the enemy to attack his lines and be destroyed by resolute and concentrated gunfire.

Longstreet rendered distinguished service at the 2nd battle of Manassas (Bull Run) though he missed a greater opportunity to destroy the Union army by attacking late in day. At the battle of Sharpsburg (Antietam) in September, Longstreet found himself again on the right flank of the army. His troops heroically held a stone bridge over Antietam Creek and prevented the Union army from crossing until battle's end. Longstreet's personal bravery at this terrible battle was well noted. Lee affectionately began to refer to Longstreet as his "old war horse."

In December, Longstreet's preferred method of making war was aptly demonstrated once again at Fredricksburg. His men, firmly entrenched on the heights above the town, were repeatedly attacked in near suicidal charges. Twelve thousand Union troops were shot down, a testament to Longstreet's faith in the rifled musket when held in steady hands.

Longstreet was sent to the James River in February 1863 and was absent from the battle of Chancellorsville. He rejoined the Army of Northern Virginia shortly thereafter and accompanied Robert E. Lee on his second invasion of the North. As the army pushed into southern Pennsylvania, it bumped into Union troops by accident at Gettysburg.

The three day battle (July 1- July 3) of Gettysburg was the "high water mark" of the Confederacy and a low point in Longstreet's career. As happened in so many of Lee's battles, Longstreet was posted on the Confederate right. On the second day of battle, his men failed to turn the Union flank as ordered, partly it is claimed, because Longstreet delayed the attack until late in the afternoon.

The controversy over Longstreet's actions on this day would continue long after his death. The debate, always heated, centered on Longstreet's disagreement with Lee over the conduct of the battle. Clearly, he knew futility of assaulting entrenched positions such as the Union troops occupied on Little Round Top and Cemetery Ridge. It was his corps, after all, that had defended Marye's Heights at Fredricksburg.

Longstreet's inability to change Lee's mind once "his blood was up" doomed the Confederate army. Lee attacked the center of the Union line on July 3rd (Pickett's Charge) with what Longstreet believed were predictable results. The Army of Northern Virginia was shattered, the tide of the war had turned. After the war, Longstreet's detractors (often Lee supporters) would point to Longstreet's performance on July 2nd and hold him accountable for the events of July 3rd.

After Gettysburg, it was clear that the Confederacy must remain on the defensive in the eastern theater. If the war was to be won, it would be won in the west where there was plenty of room to maneuver. Accordingly, Longstreet and a large body of troops were sent by rail to Chattanooga in September. Once there, they played a crucial role in the southern victory at the battle of Chickamauga. Longstreet's men pierced the center of the Union lines much as Lee had hoped to do at Gettysburg. But except for a failed attempt to take Knoxville late in 1863, Longstreet's sojourn in the west was over.

Longstreet had fallen out of favor back in Richmond. His criticism of fellow officers, failure at Gettysburg, and recent defeat outside Knoxville turned many against him. Curiously, Lee was one of a few officers who still wanted him. Though Longstreet had desperately wanted to get away from Lee after Gettysburg, he realized that his greatest successes had taken place while a member of Lee's staff. He hurriedly returned to Virginia.

In May, while serving with Lee during the Wilderness campaign, Longstreet was shot through the neck. Gravely wounded, Longstreet was carried off the field and turned his corps over to General R.H Anderson. Six months of recuperation passed before he could return to duty. In that time, however, Grant had pushed Lee back to the gates of Richmond, thrown his army over the James River and laid siege to Petersburg. There was little for Longstreet to do now but await the inevitable.

After the war, James Longstreet settled in New Orleans. He was vilified for his public view that the South should accept its defeat and quickly work itself back into the social fabric of the nation. Even worse, in some minds, Longstreet became a Republican and personal friend to U.S. Grant. In 1880, Grant appointed him Minister to Turkey. From 1897 until his death, he served as commissioner of Pacific railroads under presidents McKinley and Roosevelt. Longstreet died on January 2nd 1904, the last Confederate general officer to do so.

Thomas Jonathan Jackson
"Stonewall"

Born on January 21st 1824 in Clarksburg (West) Virginia, Thomas J. Jackson, better known to history as "Stonewall" Jackson, is one of the most revered Generals of the American Civil War. His reputation for victory earned him the respect of his peers and the loyalty of his men. Though eccentric and given to strange notions, Jackson was a dependable officer and natural leader. After being wounded at the battle of Chancellorsville, Robert E. Lee said of Jackson, "He has lost his left arm, but I have lost my right."

Thomas Jackson graduated from West Point in 1846, seventeenth in a class that would eventually produce twenty-four general officers. He fought in the Mexican American war with distinction and was promoted to the brevet rank of Major. In 1852, Jackson resigned from active duty to become an instructor at the Virginia Military Institute (VMI).

Upon Virginia's secession in April 1861, the Governor appointed Jackson to the rank of Colonel and sent him to Harper's Ferry in the Shenandoah Valley. It was Virginia's first military appointment of the war. After winning a small engagement at Falling Waters, Jackson was promoted to Brigadier General and given command of a brigade. The legend of "Stonewall" Jackson, however, would not begin until later that month.

The first major test between North and South came at the battle of Manassas (Bull Run) in July 1861. There, a green Confederate army collided with an equally green Union army advancing south toward Richmond. Popular legend has it that at a critical moment, when the battle appeared lost, General Barnard E. Bee rallied his men by pointing to Jackson and shouting, "Look men, there is Jackson …standing like a stonewall." Bee died soon thereafter, but the name stuck. The example of Jackson's brigade, steady in the face of enemy fire, was enough for the men to hold their ground. The South won the day.

Within months of the victory at Manassas, Jackson was again promoted. Now a Major General, he was sent back to the Shenandoah

Valley with orders to make a nuisance of himself and his men. Every Union regiment he could divert to the Valley meant one less regiment available to march on Richmond. Reinforced by the men of the "stonewall brigade," he soon went to work.

Jackson's "Valley Campaign" during the spring of 1862 was brilliant. Despite being outnumbered, his men fought three separate armies and won four out of five engagements. Ultimately, his command tied up 70,000 Union troops that were badly needed elsewhere. In the space of ten weeks, his troops marched the length of the Shenandoah several times. They moved so fast that they took to calling themselves Jackson's "Foot Cavalry."

Back in Washington, his success prompted fears that he might suddenly strike out of the Valley toward the capitol. To deal with this possibility, two Union armies were sent into the valley to drive him out. Not only did Jackson defeat both armies (one at Cross Keys on June 8th and the other at Port Republic on June 9th), he joined forces with Lee and drove McClellan from the gates of Richmond.

To get this kind of performance, Jackson drove his men past the point of exhaustion. He was a hard task-master and a stickler for military discipline. Though his manner was intense, he was not totally without humor. Having learned that a particular officer known for "gold-bricking" had been wounded, Jackson replied, "Wounded, you say? It must have been from an accidental discharge of duty."

Officers close to Jackson swore that he had a particular fondness for battle. They took to calling him "Old Bluelight" because of the way his blue eyes would "light" up when in combat. They noticed other strange things about the General as well. A pious man, he neither drank, smoked, or used profane language. Instead, Jackson constantly sucked on lemons, some say, to cure a hypochondriac "nervous" stomach.

With McClellan's Peninsula campaign at an end, a new threat emerged. General John Pope was moving on Richmond overland from Washington. Ironically, Pope was more or less following the same route taken by McDowell in 1861. Jackson's men, well in front of Lee and the rest of the army, delayed the Union advance near Manassas. After withstanding six frontal assaults on August 29th, Jackson was finally joined by Longstreet and Lee who counterattacked on following day. The Union army was forced to retreat. The 2nd battle of Manassas, just like its predecessor, was a Confederate victory.

Those in Jackson's corps who counted on some well deserved rest were sorely disappointed. Though they had been fighting almost non-stop since leaving the Valley in June, Jackson was ordered to capture the Union supply depot at Harper's Ferry as part of a general invasion of the North. On September 15th, Jackson accepted the mass surrender of the Harper's Ferry (12,000 men) garrison. It would be the largest surrender of American fighting men until April 9th, 1942 when 40,000 of our troops in the Philippines surrendered to the Japanese at Battaan.

With Harper's Ferry safely in Confederate hands, Jackson hurriedly marched his corps to Sharpsburg where Lee was facing the bulk of the Union army. Lee had Jackson position his troops on the Confederate left flank. On the morning of the 17th, the battle of Sharpsburg (Antietam) commenced with a massive attack on Jackson's weary troops. For the next several hours, they would find themselves engaged in a see-saw fight with two Union corps inside a forty acre cornfield.

Sharpsburg was a turning point and the single most bloody day of the American Civil War. Jackson's men held their positions despite fearsome losses but Lee's army was wrecked. On the day following the battle, the Army of Northern Virginia began its long retreat, a mere shadow of its former self. Only McClellan's poor generalship allowed it to cross over the Potomac unmolested. By November, the army was back in Virginia, firmly entrenched along the Rappahannock River at Fredericksburg.

The Union army, now led by General Ambrose Burnside, occupied the town of Fredericksburg in early December. On the 13th of the month, Burnside launched a dozen attacks on the Confederate troops holding the high ground above the town. Though the attacks had little chance for success, they came closest to breaking through near Prospect Hill, a position held by Jackson's corps. The severe losses at Fredericksburg compelled the Union army to withdraw and Burnside to resign.

His replacement, General "Fighting Joe" Hooker, resumed the advance on Richmond in March 1863. In the process of outflanking Lee, Hooker himself was flanked by Jackson's fast moving "foot cavalry." The resulting battle of Chancellorsville was Lee's most daring gamble of the war. Sending Jackson around the enemy flank involved dividing his army in the face of an already numerically superior opponent. The bold move paid off. Jackson's men hit the Union right flank and sent it reeling back in great disorder.

In four days of heavy fighting, the Union army was driven off with heavy losses. Confederate losses had been almost as high but it was the loss of one man that affected Lee the most. On May 2nd 1863, while making a reconnaissance of the front lines after dark, Jackson was accidentally shot by his own pickets. The wounds were severe enough to warrant the amputation of his left arm.

For a time it appeared that the operation was successful, the wounds were serious but not thought to be life threatening. Within the week, however, Jackson contracted pneumonia and took a turn for the worse. On May 10th 1863, a Sunday, with his wife at his side, he uttered the words, "Let us cross over the river, and rest under the shade of the trees", then died.